101 SAXOPHONE TIPS

STUFF ALL THE PROS KNOW AND USE

BY ERIC J. MORONES

ISBN 0-634-06913-6

HAL•LEONARD®
CORPORATION

7777 W. BLUEMOUND RD. P.O. BOX 13819 MILWAUKEE, WI 53213

In Australia Contact:
Hal Leonard Australia Pty. Ltd.
22 Taunton Drive P.O. Box 5130
Cheltenham East, 3192 Victoria, Australia
Email: ausadmin@halleonard.com

Visit Hal Leonard Online at
www.halleonard.com

PREFACE

In music, a true musician knows that no matter what level he or she is at there is always a limitless amount of knowledge that can be attained! This can be passed down from hearsay and/or gained through private lessons, books, or the classroom. This book is designed to give tips to the ever-seeking saxophonist (at any level) looking to find some "golden nuggets" of information. I hope that there are tips included here that can be helpful to you, whether you are a beginner at day one or a seasoned professional! Enjoy.

TABLE OF CONTENTS

Tip		Page	CD Track
1	Find the Right Reed	6	
2	Stop Sticky Pads	7	
3	Teeth Patches	7	
4	Good Finger Technique	8	
5	Ligatures	8	
6	"Stuff It"	9	
7	Key-Spring Tension	9	
8	Jaw-Dropping	9	1
9	Metal vs. Rubber	10	2–3
10	Building Vibrato	11	4
11	Organize Your Practice	12	
12	Sound Bad = Good Practice	12	
13	Multiphonics	13	5
14	Harmonic Minor Scale	13	6
15	Harmonic Minor Lick	14	7–8
16	Interval Training	14	9
17	Play With a Tuner	15	
18	Taking the Lead	15	
19	Playing Second Alto	15	
20	Record Yourself	16	
21	Build Your Music Library	16	
22	Buy Solo Transcriptions	16	
23	Get a Leak Light	17	
24	Find a Good Repairperson	17	
25	Is Your Reed Sealing?	18	
26	Fix Warped Reeds	19	
27	Avoid Squeaks	19	
28	Listen to All Styles	20	
29	Set Up a Home Studio	20	
30	Know Your Major Scales	20	
31	Blues Scales	21	10
32	Many Blues Forms	21	11
33	"Bird Blues"	22	12
34	Growling	22	13
35	Horn Hygiene	23	
36	Get Horn Insurance	23	
37	Sax in the Back Seat	23	
38	Reed Guards	23	
39	ii–V–I Progression	24	14
40	ii–V–I Pattern	25	15
41	Join a Band	25	
42	Play, Play, Play	25	
43	Mile-High Horn	26	
44	Give Your Neck a Break	26	
45	Get a Good Sax Stand	27	
46	Do Your Homework	28	
47	"Doubles" Your Pleasure	28	
48	Own Several Music Stands	28	
49	Read the Changes	29	

Tip		Page	CD Track
50	Swing It!	30	16
51	Get a Stage Microphone	30	
52	Doodle Tonguing	31	17
53	Subscribe to Music Magazines	31	
54	Study with Several Teachers	31	
55	Practice Overtones	32	18
56	Playing Low Notes	32	19
57	Hitting the High Notes	33	
58	High-Note Fingerings	33	
59	High-Note Exercise	34	20
60	The Collector's Piece!	34	
61	Always Use a Metronome	35	
62	Choose the Right Mouthpiece	35	
63	Mouthpiece Anatomy	36	
64	Don't Be a Copycat	36	
65	Train Your Ears	37	21
66	Practice Hard Scales First	37	
67	How to Practice Tunes	37	
68	Practice Changes with a Piano	38	22
69	The Mouthpiece Cap	38	
70	The Scoop	38	23
71	Buy Music Play-Alongs	39	
72	Duck Calls?	39	24
73	Get Some Earplugs	40	
74	Keep a Pencil in Your Case	40	
75	Shed the Sweet Tooth	40	
76	"The Eternal Triangle"	41	25–26
77	Tonguing It All	42	27
78	Hello, My Name Is ...	42	
79	Reed Adjustment	43	
80	Breathe Correctly	43	
81	Take "Giant Steps"	44	28
82	Choose the Right Case	45	
83	Palm Keys	45	
84	Try Stronger Reeds	46	
85	Playing Fast	46	29
86	Play What You Hear	47	30
87	Protect the Neck	47	
88	Try a New Neck	47	
89	Transcribe Solos	48	
90	Quit Your Jawing	48	
91	Studio Sessions	48	
92	Mind Your Minors	49	31–33
93	Neck Straps	50	
94	Learn How to Transpose	50	
95	Practice Softly	50	34
96	Practice Long Tones	51	35
97	Buying a Professional Horn	51	
98	ID, Please	52	
99	Build Your Repertoire	52	
100	Don't Blow These Off	52	
101	Safe Sax	53	

1 FIND THE RIGHT REED

Finding the right reed can be difficult, especially since there are dozens of brand names, strengths, and cuts from which to choose. Here are some tips to finding the right reed:

A. Find a brand of reed that gives you the sound you want. Every brand offers its own strengths and cuts, and they all sound different, depending on the type of mouthpiece you use. Find the one that sounds best to your ears.

B. The reed should be yellow or golden in color. Strange discolorations like pale, sandy, white-beige, or green should be avoided.

C. Hold the reed up to the light and look for an even, upside-down "U" shape in the middle of the reed. This is called the "heart." If the "U" is not even, or if there's no dark center, this usually means the reed has no depth and probably will not play well.

D. The "butt" of the reed bark should be about 1" thick and cut evenly on both sides. If not, air might leak from the sides when you play.

E. Find a reed that has a lot of fibers running up and down its length.

F. Avoid plastic or plastic-covered reeds. Some people use these for their consistency and longevity, but plastic lacks the warmth, intonation, and sound quality of real cane.

G. Make sure the reed strength goes with your mouthpiece. A harder reed doesn't mean anything as far as playing level or "hipness." Your mouthpiece tip opening may require a soft reed. Worry about the reed strength only for the purposes of tone quality.

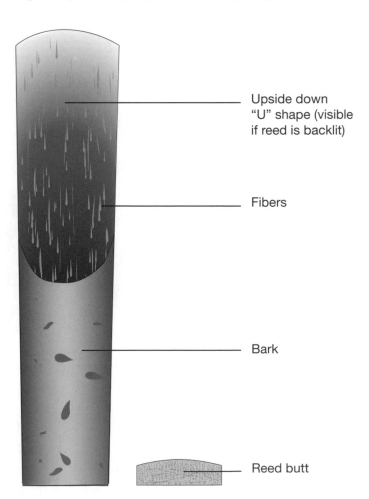

Upside down
"U" shape (visible
if reed is backlit)

Fibers

Bark

Reed butt

② STOP STICKY PADS

Sticky pads are the result of moisture and dirt build-up on the pad. They are annoying anytime you play, but especially on a gig or right before a recital. For a quick remedy, some people place a dollar bill between the pad and the keyhole, press the key against the bill, hold it down for a few seconds, and then release it. This works fine in a pinch, but usually doesn't last very long. For a more permanent fix, try a product like Yamaha Powder Paper. With this type of product, a fine powder residue is left on the pad, thus leaving the pad stick-free.

Another quick remedy: lick and soak a piece of paper with your saliva, large enough to cover the pad. Now, while covering the pad with the wet paper and holding the key down, tear off the paper around the key, and leave it on over the pad. Remove any excess paper that runs over the pad. The paper should stick on the pad. Leave it there and continue to play with the paper over the sticky pad.

Always avoid using soap, rubbing alcohol, or other cleaning materials on the pads, since these materials will dry out the pads.

③ TEETH PATCHES

Mouthpiece teeth patches primarily help prevent horn vibration on your teeth. They can also provide a steady mouth position on the mouthpiece, as well as make a difference in the "feel" of the instrument. They can be bought in packs, and you can cut the patches in half to double the quantity.

Another way, instead of buying teeth patches, is to use black electrical tape. First, wash the mouthpiece with warm water and dish soap to remove oil or dirt from the mouthpiece beak (this will help the tape stay on longer). Then, cut two pieces of electrical tape (enough to cover the beak of the mouthpiece) and stack them on top of one another. *Voilà!* You now have your own homemade mouthpiece patches!

4 GOOD FINGER TECHNIQUE

Developing good saxophone technique is very important at any level. It helps you play music smoother, cleaner, and faster. Always make sure your fingers are curved, relaxed, and close to each other on the keys.

A good trick to help develop proper finger technique is to try holding a pen or pencil between your fingers while you play—without "dropping" it. This forces you to keep your fingers close, relaxed, and curved. Try it!

5 LIGATURES

Ligatures serve one purpose: to hold the reed on the mouthpiece. But this very important job makes a huge difference in your sound.

There are dozens of ligatures on the market with prices ranging from $5 to $70. Do they make a difference? Yes, they do. Ligatures also provide certain pressure points on the reed, which makes it vibrate in different ways and areas. Experiment with several ligatures and note the difference each makes on your sound, volume, and tone quality. An inexpensive $5 ligature actually might sound better than the $70 one; use your own ears to decide.

"STUFF IT"

"Stuff It" Pad Savers leave fuzz and dust between your keys, inside the horn, and inside your case. Stick with a standard cleaning swab wiped throughout the horn.

If you do decide to use a "Stuff It" Pad Saver, don't leave it inside the horn while in the case. Use it to wipe through the horn a couple of times, and then leave it in the case outside of the horn. You'll still get fuzz and dust in your case and on the keys, but not as much as you would from "stuffing" it in the horn.

KEY-SPRING TENSION

The way the action "feels" on a horn (light or heavy) depends on the key-spring tension. If you don't like the action of the keys, you can adjust the springs yourself—if you're careful.

First, undo the needle-like spring on the key, and then carefully remove the key that you wish to adjust. The spring tension increases or decreases by bending the spring in one direction or the other. If you want to increase the key tension, bend the spring away from the key and toward the body of the horn. If you want to decrease the tension, bend the spring toward the key and away from the body of the horn. You can use a pencil with an eraser head, a small tweezers, or a small crochet needle (this is best, because of its hook) to do this. Be careful not to bend or push the spring too much, or you will break it.

When you're finished with the adjustment, put the key back on and try it out. If you still don't like the tension, repeat the previous steps. If nothing seems to work, you may need to take it to a repairperson to replace the spring altogether. And remember, certain keys need to have a particular level of tension to work.

If you don't feel comfortable doing any of this yourself, go to a repairperson to do it for you; this is always the best way.

JAW-DROPPING

Your personal sound comes from your embouchure, mouth design, throat, air stream, tongue position, and, of course, the reed-mouthpiece combination. But another important part of your sound is making sure the reed vibrates to its fullest capacity.

Practice dropping your lower jaw, thus allowing the reed to vibrate more when you play, and listen to how the sound "opens up." You'll be surprised at just how much difference this maneuver makes! Play some long tones while dropping your jaw to help strengthen your embouchure muscles. If your embouchure starts to tire, it means you're exercising and working the muscles properly, so keep going!

Listen to Track 1 to hear how the sound "opens up" just by dropping the jaw.

TRACK 1

9 METAL VS. RUBBER

Finding the right mouthpiece can be a huge search. And choosing between a hard-rubber or a metal mouthpiece can be even tougher because of the differences between the two. Here are some differences:

METAL

Many of today's R&B or smooth-jazz artists commonly use metal mouthpieces. Metal's hard, clear, edgy, robust, aggressive tone sounds good on tenor and baritone saxophones, but you should avoid using them on altos, unless you're going for that type of tone. Further, beginning students should probably avoid metal until they have developed a strong embouchure on the instrument. Otherwise, you'll notice that reeds will tend to squeak more.

Some popular metal mouthpieces include Otto Link, Dukoff, Berg Larson, Beechler, Guardala, Sugal, Ponzol, and Yanagasawa. More expensive than hard rubber, these range in price from $100–$600.

HARD RUBBER

Overall, hard rubber is a better mouthpiece material than metal. It's warmer, smoother, less robust, less edgy, and easier to control. For all these reasons, it's better for beginners. Many jazz artists use hard rubber on the alto saxophone, yet few use it on the tenor. Some popular hard-rubber mouthpieces include Berg Larson, Meyer, Selmer, Vandoren, and Morgan. These typically cost between $50 and $200.

Remember that the style of music you're going to play is an important issue when deciding the type of mouthpiece you should use. You really wouldn't want to play classical music with a Dukoff metal mouthpiece! As always, use your ears to decide what type of mouthpiece gives you the sound you want. If you're still not sure, ask a fellow sax player for advice.

Using major scales and the melody below, Tracks 2 and 3 show the tonal difference between metal and hard-rubber mouthpieces:

TRACK 2
hard rubber

TRACK 3
metal

10 BUILDING VIBRATO

Vibrato is the constant, even fluctuation of pitch; its parameters are speed and intensity. It can be used on long, sustained notes or during fast-moving melodies. Whether you want a classical or a jazz vibrato, it's the same concept.

There are two types of vibrato on the saxophone: *triplet* vibrato and *sixteenth-note* vibrato. To practice vibrato, set your metronome to quarter note=60 bpm.

First, play triplet vibrato evenly for four beats.

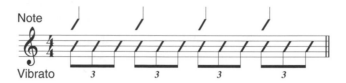

Make sure the "waves" of the vibrato are even—not jagged or inconsistent. Next, play some major scales in this fashion.

Now, move on to sixteenth-note vibrato. You should exaggerate your jaw movement in the beginning; look in the mirror to help. Make sure the waves are smooth and even.

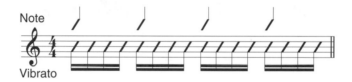

When you feel like you can perform both vibratos evenly at the slow tempo, gradually increase the tempo. This is how you'll build faster yet even vibrato. If your embouchure gets tired, keep going! This means you're working your chin muscles. Try to devote some time for vibrato every time you practice!

To hear a good example of both vibrato types, listen to the following scale as played on Track 4.

TRACK 4

11 ORGANIZE YOUR PRACTICE

Be more organized with your practice routine, and you'll be surprised at how more productive you can be. First, decide the total time you're going to dedicate to practice. Then divide your time evenly to work on several things instead of just one. Keep a notebook for tracking how much time you've devoted to each topic, exactly what you practiced, and how long you practiced it. Be very specific, including dates and times, right down to the minute.

If you're not sure how to start, here are a few practice ideas: Begin with long tones, followed by some scales (starting with the hard keys). Then work on patterns, book etudes or passages, solo transcriptions, sight reading, learning tunes, vibrato exercises, and other technique challenges. Make sure to devote some time to new things as well. This will help keep your practice routine fresh and new. Try to keep a daily practice schedule, too. It's better to practice a little bit every day than it is to practice once every five days!

12 SOUND BAD = GOOD PRACTICE

One of the main purposes of practicing is to work on things that you don't know yet. Sometimes, our egos get in the way, and we want the people around us to hear us sound good the whole time. But if you're *really* practicing, you should sound bad! If you sound too good, that means you're probably playing something you already know. If you work on the tough stuff without worrying about sounding bad, you'll get better with faster results!

13 MULTIPHONICS

Multiphonics occur when you play two or more pitches simultaneously. John Coltrane and Eric Dolphy were two jazz greats who've mastered this technique, and many modern players like David Sanborn use them on high notes.

There are certain fingerings that are used to get the multiphonic effect. Since there are tons of fingerings for all the notes, I'll just give a couple of examples.

A. As you finger a low B♭, open the G key on your left hand and play the note. Try to keep your embouchure still when you hear the two notes at the same time. If you can't get the effect, experiment with your mouth and throat cavity to achieve it.

B. As you finger low B, open the A key on your left hand and play the note.

TRACK 5

For more on multiphonics, check out *Multiphonics for Saxophone* by John Gross. This book contains over 100 different fingerings and suggestions.

14 HARMONIC MINOR SCALE

The harmonic minor scale comes from the sixth mode or note of a major scale and has a raised 7th note. It has been used in compositions of all styles. In jazz, it is especially effective when applied over a minor ii–V–i progression (see Tip 39). Here's an example of how you build a harmonic minor scale from an E♭ major scale. First, start with the E♭ major scale:

E♭ major scale

Now go to the sixth note, C, and play the notes of the E♭ major scale starting on C. This is the sixth mode of E♭ major, also called C Aeolian (or C natural minor):

Now, to create a harmonic minor from this scale, just raise the 7th note, B♭, by one half step, to B natural:

And there it is: the C harmonic minor scale! Track 6 demonstrates what a C harmonic minor scale sounds like.

TRACK 6

15 HARMONIC MINOR LICK

Now that you know what a harmonic minor scale is and how it sounds, let's learn a pattern and where to apply it. Mentioned in Tip 14, we learned that the harmonic minor scale can be played over minor ii–V–i progressions. Here is what a minor ii–V–i looks and sounds like:

Now, using the C harmonic minor scale, play a pattern over the progression. Whatever the i chord is, use that scale over the whole progression. In this example, the i chord is Cm7, so we will use the C harmonic minor scale.

Learn the harmonic minor scale in all 12 keys, and practice this pattern in all keys, too.

16 INTERVAL TRAINING

Intervals are the movements or pitch differences between two notes. Practicing intervals is great for your technique, ear training, and music theory. Take a major scale and practice it in diatonic intervals as shown. Practice playing and hearing these intervals in all 12 keys.

TRACK 9

17 PLAY WITH A TUNER

Playing in tune is very important, especially when playing with other people. So you should get into the habit of *always* practicing with a tuner. If you don't own a tuner, run out and buy one right now! Inexpensive tuners can cost around $20, with fancy ones ranging all the way up to $200. Make sure it's one that tells you if you're too sharp or too flat, not one that just gives you a pitch to match.

When playing with a tuner for the first time, you may be surprised at how out-of-tune you are. The tuner never lies! Find out what notes on the horn are out of tune and practice adjusting your embouchure to play them in tune. Also find the correct mouthpiece placement on the neck cork to help limit embouchure adjustments.

18 TAKING THE LEAD

Playing lead alto in a big band section (or any section) requires a strong tone with volume that will cut through the horn section, and many times, even the whole band. Make sure you have a professional-quality horn, a bright mouthpiece that plays in tune with projection, and have style characteristics like cut-offs, bends, song interpretation, and vibrato down confidently. As the lead alto player, you set the stage for what the horn section should do to make the section sound like one. Be confident and in control!

19 PLAYING SECOND ALTO

Playing second alto also requires a good, strong tone that accents the lead alto's lines and style. There are many times in harmony parts where the second alto's part needs to be louder than the lead alto. You not only must be able to play in tune with the lead alto, but also be able to follow the cut-offs, bends, vibrato, and style interpretations that the lead alto plays. Also, you need to know when to back off on the volume to allow the lead to cut more, as well as when to play louder than the lead player when your part is more exposed. Remember that the second alto's part is just as important as that of the lead.

20 RECORD YOURSELF

Get in the habit of recording yourself—often! It can be quite scary to hear yourself for the first time, but the tape doesn't lie. It reveals what you *really* sound like. I guarantee that after the first time you hear yourself on tape, you will think, "I sound like *that*?" Listen for your sound quality, time problems, intonation, and other noticeable flaws. A good microphone and tape player will reveal things you've never noticed before.

When you do record yourself practicing, make note of the problems that you hear so you can correct them later. When you are finished with the tapes, mark and date them, and store them somewhere safe. Then, months—or even years—later, you can go back and listen to what you sounded like. Hopefully, you'll sound better!

21 BUILD YOUR MUSIC LIBRARY

All serious musicians have huge collections of records, CDs, songbooks, and sheet music. You should start your own library of music, too! Start collecting records and CDs to have a big reference of music on hand. You should own all of the famous "required" jazz recordings, recordings of famous classical pieces, and selections from all styles of music from the '20s to today. Then, buy some corresponding songbooks of the music you have for study and analysis. For example, buy a Beatles songbook to analyze what makes their songs so great and popular. The same goes for sheet music from the pop hits of today. Sure, some of it is nonsense, but understanding why it's popular can give you some insight into how to incorporate those characteristics into your own playing or writing. Having a diverse musical background and wide-ranging tastes only makes you a better musician!

22 BUY SOLO TRANSCRIPTIONS

Purchase some transcription books of solos that you like as well as ones for which you have the recordings. These books will save you the time and effort of transcribing the solos yourself (see Tip 89).

When learning to play a solo transcription, first practice the solo away from the recording with a metronome, working on correct articulations, nuances, and phrasing. Once you've got the solo under your fingers, speed up the tempo. Next, get the recording of the solo or song and try to play along with it note for note. Playing along with the recording will help your phrasing, articulation, and technique tremendously! Find some cool patterns or licks that you like in the solo, learn them, and practice them in all twelve keys!

23 GET A LEAK LIGHT

Leaks on your horn are the result of wear on the pads, and possibly from a dented tone hole. If you do have a leak, you'll notice some intonation problems, squeaks, or even notes that don't come out. You can check for leaks by closing the key and doing an "eye spot check." If you see even the smallest hairline opening between the pad and tone hole, there's a leak, and it will have to be fixed.

A sure way to spot leaks is to use a leak light. Every saxophonist should own one. They're pretty inexpensive, and you can periodically check your horn(s). You can buy one from your local music store or distributor, or you can make your own using white Christmas tree lights. The way to use a leak light is as follows: First, go into a dark room and turn off the lights. Then, put the light through the horn and close the keys where you believe the leak may be. If light slips through the pad and tone hole, there's a leak. Take it to a good repairperson to be fixed.

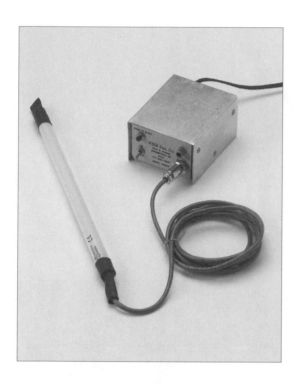 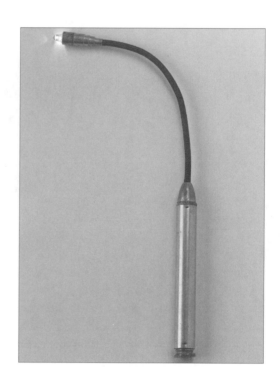

24 FIND A GOOD REPAIRPERSON

Would you send your child to a bad doctor? I didn't think so. Your horn is your baby, so you should find a repairperson that you can trust. Ask other musicians or someone at your local music store to find out which repairpersons have good reputations. If they specialize in saxophone repairs, or play the sax themselves, that's even better! Your repairperson is someone you should trust, someone who is serious about his or her work, someone who makes you feel comfortable when you have questions, and finally, someone who won't make any changes to your horn without your approval. Find this person, and your horn will be in great hands!

25 IS YOUR REED SEALING?

Making sure your reed is sealing to the mouthpiece is very important. This not only helps to avoid squeaks, but also makes sure your reed is vibrating and responding evenly on the mouthpiece, and checks that no air is leaking out of the sides of the reed. To check for a proper seal, try a pop test.

Take your mouthpiece with the reed on it and put the "barrel" part over your hand, covering the hole tightly. Try to suck the air out of the mouthpiece, making the reed "close up" at the mouthpiece tip opening. After holding itself closed for a few seconds, the reed should make a "pop" noise when the air comes out. If it's not sealing at all, or if it pops too quickly, this means air is leaking out of the sides of the rails, and the reed is not sealing properly. Usually, this is a sign of a bad reed, but it sometimes means that there are problems with the mouthpiece rails. Check the mouthpiece rails for any chips or cracks. If they are fine, then replace the reed with a new one.

You can also use the pop test to iron out warped reeds. (See Tip 26).

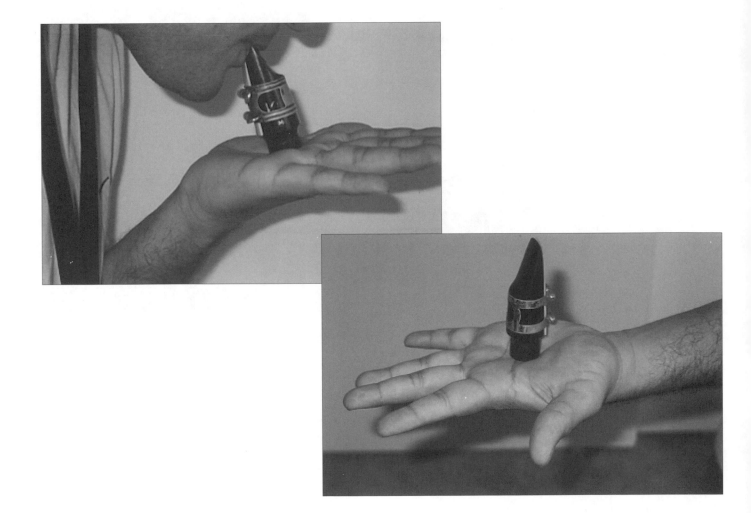

26 FIX WARPED REEDS

Warped reeds are the result of the reed cane drying out. You can tell that your reed is warped if it squeaks, sounds too airy, or has a warped look to it. To keep a reed from becoming warped, be sure to properly dry it when you finish playing, and then keep it in a good reed holder. Also, soaking the reed in water for a couple of minutes before playing is known to help. If you find that your reed is still warped, the pop test from Tip 25 might help.

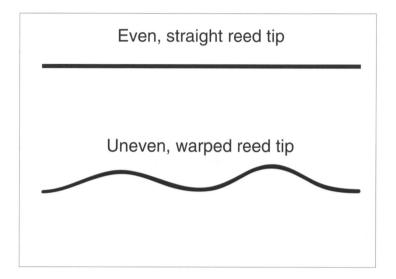

27 AVOID SQUEAKS

Squeaks can be the result of several things: a bad reed, a reed not sealing, or a problem with the horn itself. As almost all squeaks come from a bad reed, the first thing to do when you have a squeak is to check for a warped reed. Do this by looking at the tip of the reed at the opening on the mouthpiece. If it's wrinkled or crooked, it's warped (see Tip 26). If it is warped, try the pop test from Tip 25 first. If this doesn't work, put on a new reed. Squeaks can also come from leaking pads or even sloppy technique! If the new reed doesn't help, see a good repairperson to find the cause of the squeak.

28 LISTEN TO ALL STYLES

Listen to all different types of music, but especially different saxophone styles. Educating yourself in all saxophone styles will make you a better musician and player. Listen to classical music, jazz, smooth jazz, bebop, swing, ska, rock 'n' roll sax, and even heavy metal sax! Purchase sheet music and recordings of the saxophone in all styles and learn them. You never know when you might need to pull off one of these styles on a gig!

29 SET UP A HOME STUDIO

Since we're living in this digital recording age, it's important to have some knowledge of recording equipment. These days, recording gear is fairly inexpensive and easy to learn and understand. You can purchase either an all-in-one desktop digital recorder, or you can install recording software on your computer. You'll also need to invest in a good microphone, a mixer, and the right cables. With the right setup, you can even burn your own CDs!

To get started, check out some home recording books or magazines to help you choose the right approach for your needs. Once you have the gear, be sure to read all the equipment manuals as well. All of this will allow you to get some valuable studio experience in your own home, which may come in handy for future recording situations you may find yourself in.

30 KNOW YOUR MAJOR SCALES

The major scale is the foundation of Western music. Our whole system of theory, chords, and keys relates back to major scales. If you don't know your major scales, it will be pretty tough to navigate most of the tunes that come across your music stand. So learn and master the major scale, practicing them ascending and descending, in 3rds, 4ths, 5ths, and 6ths, in all 12 keys. Like the saying goes, "There are no hard keys, just keys you don't know!"

31 BLUES SCALES

The blues is a style of music that goes way back to the mid-1800s. Today, it's still very popular and fun to play. The standard blues form contains 12 bars (see Tip 32). While playing over the blues form, you can play a specific blues scale to match the song's key. For example, if you're playing a blues in G, you could play a G blues scale throughout the whole song.

The blues scale is a six-note scale that contains the root, ♭3rd, 4th, ♭5th, 5th, and ♭7th. Below, you'll find the G and C blues scales spelled out for you ascending and descending, and played straight and with a "swing feel" on the track.

TRACK 10

Remember, there is a blues scale for every key. Try to learn all 12!

32 MANY BLUES FORMS

Now that we know what a blues scale is, let's see where to apply it! The 12-bar blues comes in many forms and progressions. You should try to learn as many of those blues progressions as you can. The example below is a standard blues form that any typical blues can have:

TRACK 11

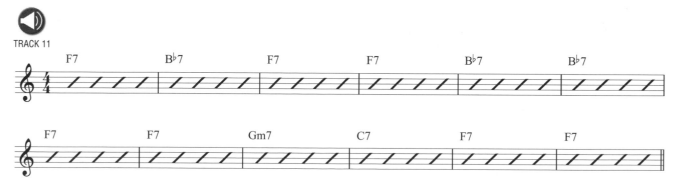

(Note: The progression above is for the key of F. You must transpose for your instrument.)

33 "BIRD BLUES"

After learning the basic blues form (Tip 32), try learning this advanced blues form called "Bird Blues." Charlie "Bird" Parker invented his own version of the 12-bar blues by incorporating his own chord changes over the basic blues form. The "Bird Blues" changes are shown below. Remember, this example is in the key of F, so you must transpose for your instrument.

TRACK 12

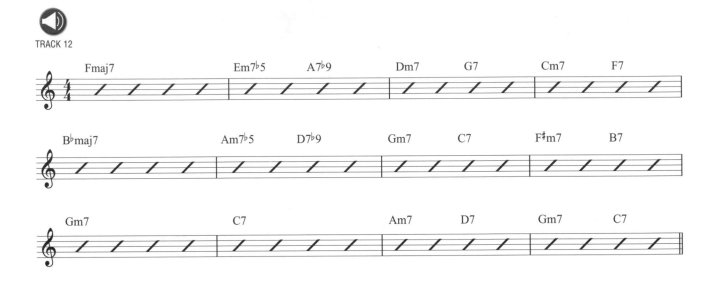

34 GROWLING

Growling is a unique technique that can add color and character to your playing. It can be used for entire musical lines or just on one note. Growling is very popular and useful in the rock 'n' roll styles of such saxophonists as Illinois Jacquet and Clarence Clemmons. Even some smooth jazz artists have been known to growl a bit.

Growling is basically achieved by humming or growling while you play. It can be hard to do at first, but with practice you'll get it. Try playing a note while you hum or growl on it. You'll notice a very interesting nuance to the note. In the beginning, or through excess use of this technique, your throat might start to hurt, so practice with caution.

Track 13 uses the following melody showing the use of growling:

TRACK 13

35 HORN HYGIENE

You should clean your horn after every time you play. This helps keep food particles, dust, dirt, and saliva out of your horn, makes the pads last longer, and helps avoid any mold buildup inside the horn. Cleaning your horn also can add years to the instrument's life.

Don't forget to clean your mouthpiece once a week with warm water and soap—inside and out. This helps prevent smelly reeds, a smelly mouthpiece, and the build-up of mold or food particles inside. Also, wash the horn's neck often. Run warm water at full blast through the neck, and watch the dirt build-up clear out!

36 GET HORN INSURANCE

Make sure to have all of your instruments insured. You never know when they may be damaged or stolen. Insurance can help for repairs too. Horn insurance is relatively cheap compared to the cost of full replacement of your horn. Sometimes, you can get a huge discount if you belong to a musician's union or ASCAP. You can also purchase horn insurance through your home insurance policy. Look on the internet or call your local musician's union to find a reputable musical instrument insurance broker.

37 SAX IN THE BACK SEAT

Instead of driving somewhere with your horns in the trunk, put them in the back seat. Many people have had their horns damaged in car accidents when they were rear-ended with their horns in the trunk. Instead, keep them in the back seat while you drive to avoid a possible horn accident.

38 REED GUARDS

Use a reed guard to protect your reeds from damage and warping. You can also use the reed guard to help keep track of the reeds you've been playing on. Buy a reed guard that can hold four reeds and number the reed slots from 1-4 (1 being your best reed). This lets you know which reed is best and fourth best. Also, you should always rotate your reeds to make them last longer, rather than playing the same reed over and over again.

39 II-V-I PROGRESSION

The ii–V–I progression is the most common chord progression in all of music (including jazz and pop). We hear this progression so often that our ears expect the ii chord to move to the V chord, and likewise the V to resolve to the I. So, what is a ii–V–I progression? Let's start with a C major scale:

If you build a chord using the root, 3rd, 5th, and 7th notes, you get a Cmaj7 chord (C–E–G–B).

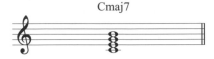

This is the I Chord.

Now, let's build the ii chord. Go to the second note of the C major scale, D, and play the notes of the C major scale starting on D. This is the D Dorian mode:

Building a chord (1–3–5–7) from this scale you get Dm7 (D–F–A–C).

This is the ii chord.

Now, from the same C major scale, go up to the 5th note, G, and play the scale starting on that note. This is the G Mixolydian mode.

Using the same 1–3–5–7 formula, you get a G7 chord (G–B–D–F), which is the V chord.

Now, take those three chords and put them in the ii–V–I order, and you have a Dm7–G7–Cmaj7 progression:

TRACK 14

40 II–V–I PATTERN

Here is a simple ii–V–I pattern composed of eighth notes. The first measure (ii chord) begins by outlining Dm7 with the D Dorian scale. The second measure (V chord) descends the G7 chord and scale, and the third measure (I chord) outlines the Cmaj7 chord.

Listen to Track 15 and practice this pattern in all 12 keys.

TRACK 15

41 JOIN A BAND

The best way to get experience and get your playing abilities together is to play with other live musicians. There are always places and opportunities to play; you just have to find them. You could join a local community or college band, or find other musicians to jam with and form your own band!

No matter what your level, you should play with anybody you can. If you're a beginner or hobbyist who doesn't play professionally, find some players like you who just want to play for fun, with no pressure or judging. You'd be surprised how many "bedroom" players are out there who would love to play anytime, anywhere! So get out there and find them!

Also, don't be afraid to play with a band that plays a different style of music from what you're used to playing. Be open to trying all different styles of music. Play with a Klezmer, country, polka, or even a mariachi band if you can. It could be fun, and it may open your ears up to new things.

42 PLAY, PLAY, PLAY

Get as much playing experience as you can! Something can be learned from every playing opportunity—be it good or bad. Don't worry about how much money a gig pays, who's playing, or where it takes place—just go and play! Not only is it a chance to play, it also gives someone a chance to hear what you sound like. You never know who might be in the audience that night! Remember, playing every chance offered is just another way to get your name out there and market yourself!

43 MILE-HIGH HORN

Traveling with your horn(s) on a plane these days can be a hassle, especially if you want to carry it with you on the plane. To make it easier, first determine if your case will be able to fit in the overhead compartment. If you play tenor or alto (or baritone, if you have a soft case), chances are you will be able carry it on. However, some airlines will want you to check it first.

If you do plan to check your horn, make sure you have a strong, sturdy case that holds your horn tightly inside the case. Bag handlers don't care what items are inside and will probably just throw it around. And if an airline does damage it, chances are they won't pay for it.

Another alternative is to bring your horn all the way to the gate, and then ask an attendant there to check it in as a "special carry-on." The attendant will give you a red tag to claim it, and then have someone walk it to the luggage-loading area to be placed in the cargo hold. When the plane arrives at your destination, you can wait on the unloading bridge, where someone actually walks your horn to you. This keeps it from going through the baggage terminal and gets your horn some extra care!

44 GIVE YOUR NECK A BREAK

During a break on a gig or at home while practicing, take the neck off the horn (with the mouthpiece still on) and put it in the bell of your saxophone. This will prevent accidental damage from other people bumping into it and accidentally bending the neck.

45 GET A GOOD SAX STAND

Purchase a good-quality, stable, folding stand for your saxophone and always use it on a gig or at home when not playing, instead of putting the horn on a chair or on the floor. The stand will protect it from being kicked or knocked over.

Make sure the stand holds the saxophone tightly at the bell, is well padded to avoid scratching the horn, and sits sturdily on the ground without rocking back and forth. If you play several horns (both tenor and alto) or doubles (see Tip 47), be sure to get a stand that can hold both horns as well as a flute and a clarinet. Get two stands if you can—one for your home or practice space, and the other to leave in your car for work!

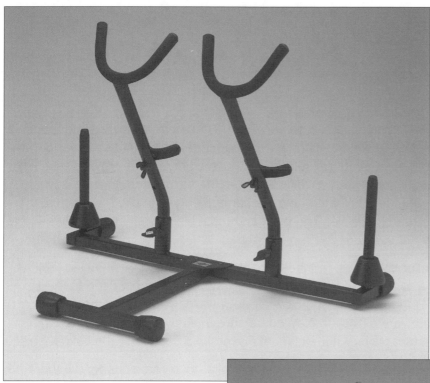

DO YOUR HOMEWORK

If you are playing a certain classical or jazz piece for a recital or gig, find a recording of the song. Listening to someone else's interpretation of the piece helps you gain insight on how the song should be played. If it's a classical piece, listen for tone quality, vibrato, dynamics, and other style reflections. If it's a jazz piece, listen to how the melody is played, how the artist adds his or her own stylistic reflections to it, and listen to how he or she solos over the tune. Make notes on your sheet music with pencil as you listen. You can even try to play along with the recording, matching what is played, and then incorporate it when you play the song.

47 "DOUBLES" YOUR PLEASURE

Trying to make a living playing only the saxophone can be very hard. That's why it's always a good idea to learn what are considered the *doubles*—flute and clarinet—to add more opportunities to your playing career. There's always the chance that some parts will require flute and clarinet to be played, especially in big band charts! While the flute and clarinet are very different from the saxophone, they do have some similarities. Several note fingerings are the same, and the same theory is applied when reading the different parts, because they all are in treble clef. The main and most difficult difference between the doubles and the saxophone is in the embouchure.

The clarinet, though it has some similar fingerings, requires a tighter, stronger embouchure, as well as more chin support, correct posture, and the need to properly cover tone holes (as opposed to the sax, where there are no holes to cover). On the clarinet, you blow air downward, whereas on the sax, you blow air straight ahead. The clarinet is very difficult to play, so be sure to study with a proper teacher. Always strive to sound like a real clarinet player—not a clarinet player who "sounds" like a saxophonist.

The flute is a different deal altogether. There are some fingerings similar to the saxophone, but there are many differences. Flute requires a strong, tight, yet flexible embouchure as well as a lot of air. Plus, it doesn't use a reed. The flute is tuned by rolling the head joint forward or backwards while playing, and you hit the high notes by squeezing the embouchure tighter. It requires a lot of practice to maintain your technique and embouchure muscles.

48 OWN SEVERAL MUSIC STANDS

Like your sax stands (see Tip 46), you should own a couple of nice music stands—one for home and another to keep in your car. You never know when you might need one on a gig or when someone else might need it (this always makes you look prepared). Wired music stands are fine, as they are cheaper and easily portable. But if possible, you should invest in a nice sturdy one with a wide lip to hold plenty of sheet music and practice materials—and don't forget to put your name on it somewhere!

49 READ THE CHANGES

Chord changes in jazz are just what they sound like; they tell an instrument like the piano or guitar what chords to play. For the saxophonist soloing with those changes, they indicate which scale to play over each particular chord. If you understand the "value" of the chord, knowing what scale will go with it is very easy. Here is some basic information on chords:

When you see a letter by itself, or written with "MA," "Maj7," or a triangle, this indicates a major chord, which requires a major scale:

The numeral "7" directly following the chord root letter (e.g., C7) indicates a dominant chord, which requires the Mixolydian mode (major scale with a ♭7th):

If you see a chord root letter followed by a lowercase "m," "m7," "-," or "-7," this indicates a minor 7th chord, over which you should play the Dorian mode (major scale with ♭3rd and ♭7th):

Other alterations to the chord, such as ♭9, ♯9, ♯4, ♭5, or ♯5, indicate that you apply that specific alteration to that particular note when you play the scale. For example, if you see a C7♯5 chord, you should play the C Mixolydian mode and substitute a G♯ (♯5) for G (5).

50 SWING IT!

Learning to play correct jazz articulation can be simple. The jazz "feel" sounds like a dotted eighth followed by a 16th-note rhythm ( ) or an eighth-note triplet with the first two eighth notes tied together ( ). To get a jazz sound on these rhythms, you just have to tongue all the upbeats. It will sound either like you're alternating tongued articulation and slurred eighth notes (Fig. 1), or like dotted eighths and sixteenth notes (Fig. 2) with slurs. The hard part is getting your tongue used to doing this and making sure it sounds smooth, with a swing feel.

Fig. 1

Fig. 2

To practice, play a G major scale in straight eighth notes. While keeping the air constantly flowing, tongue every other note. Sometimes it helps to tap your foot while playing the eighth notes; this reminds you to tongue the upbeats. Practice slowly with a metronome, and then increase the tempo. Also, listen to famous jazz artists to hear how they articulate their notes in this manner.

TRACK 16

51 GET A STAGE MICROPHONE

Carry an inexpensive stage microphone with you to gigs. The venue might be bigger than you expected, or perhaps the volume of the ensemble will overwhelm you. In cases like these, a good, reliable, all-purpose microphone such as the Shure SM-58 can be a gig-saver. You can pick one up for around $100 or less. It can be used for vocals or as a recording mic as well.

You can assume that there will be a mixer, monitor, and power amp at the gig, but don't forget to have a long microphone cable and a microphone stand.

52 DOODLE TONGUING

Doodle tonguing is a technique in which you use your tongue to make fast lines sound smoother, cleaner, and more *legato*. You do this by holding or leaving your tongue on the reed while you play through the notes. It's a technique that's been in practice since the bebop era (saxophonist Charlie Parker used it on his double-time lines), and many trombonists today use a similar technique. Try doodle tonguing for this famous Charlie Parker line:

TRACK 17

53 SUBSCRIBE TO MUSIC MAGAZINES

Periodicals can be a great source of information. They can come monthly, weekly, or bi-monthly, and are devoted to every aspect of music. Consider subscribing to those that are geared specifically toward the saxophone, as well as those that focus on the music industry, music equipment, or songwriting. And make sure that you always save them, so you can refer to past articles when necessary. You'll find that the magazines can be a great source of information and study for many years, especially as you improve and grow as a player!

54 STUDY WITH SEVERAL TEACHERS

Study and play with as many different musicians you can. Every player or teacher has his or her own ideas, views, concepts, advice, and methods of playing. Gather as many of these concepts as you can, decide which ones you like, and then incorporate them into your own playing.

Believe it or not, some famous players occasionally offer lessons. Try to take advantage of these opportunities if you can. But realize that these celebrity lessons may come with a price. But isn't it worth paying $100 for an hour-long lesson with a famous player if you'll get something from that player that you can't get elsewhere? It sure is! If you do get the opportunity with one of these lessons, don't be afraid to ask a lot of questions, no matter how silly or elementary you think they are.

55 PRACTICE OVERTONES

Overtones are a fantastic way to help with your tone production—and a must for playing high (altissimo) notes. Basically, you produce overtones by playing a note, and then making subtle throat adjustments to produce a higher note(s), all while using the same fingering. For example, have you ever tried to play a low B♭ only to have the B♭ one octave higher sound? That's an overtone.

To practice overtones, finger the B♭ notated on the 3rd line of the treble clef. As you play the note, drop to the fingering of low B♭ but try to keep the same pitch. Notice any subtle changes in your throat and don't pinch with your lip. If you have trouble, try the following: while your throat is in the normal "ah" position, drop it to an "oh" position to help with the overtone.

For the following exercise, play a low B♭ without the octave key, and then, go for the B♭ one octave above. Next, go for the next higher F note, followed by B♭ two octaves above the low B♭, and so on. You can hear it performed properly on Track 18. Practice this exercise daily, and when you're ready, move on to low B and C, with their respective overtones. Remember that you can only play altissimo notes if you can play overtones well!

TRACK 18

56 PLAYING LOW NOTES

Low notes can be the hardest notes to play on the saxophone. Here are some tips to help:

- Remember to use a softer reed.
- Angle your air downward into the mouthpiece.
- Relax your embouchure.
- Keep your jaw and mouth cavity still.
- Make sure to finger the note cleanly; sloppy technique can prevent notes from coming out.
- Try to play a low B several times perfectly. Pay attention to what your embouchure is doing when you are able to play the note successfully several times.

A good exercise is to play a middle D, then drop to the lower D without moving your jaw, making sure it's a clean change between the notes. After D, then go to C, dropping to the low C, and continue descending to low B♭. Make sure it's a clean movement between the notes.

Another exercise is to play chromatically from low B♭ up to low D with a clean, full tone, making each note clear. This also will help build your low-note technique.

TRACK 19

HITTING THE HIGH NOTES

Playing high, or altissimo, notes on the saxophone requires a strong embouchure, strong reed, a quality mouthpiece, and the correct high-note fingerings. A great way to learn how to play high notes is to first practice overtones (Tip 55). Then, when you're comfortable producing overtones, give some high-note fingerings a try!

 **HIGH-NOTE FINGERINGS**

Here are some fingerings for notes above high F for alto and tenor sax. Some of these fingerings will work; some won't. Also, some will be in tune, and again, some won't. Choose ones that work best for you and your horn.

ALTO With Octave Key

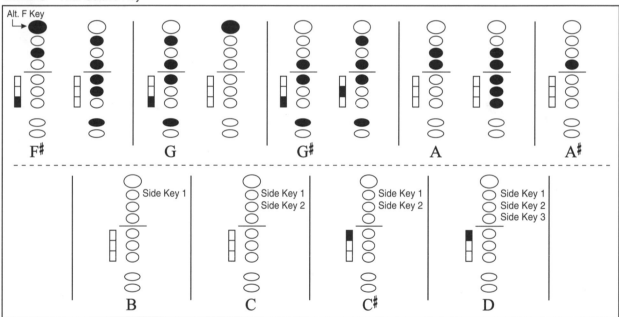

TENOR With Octave Key

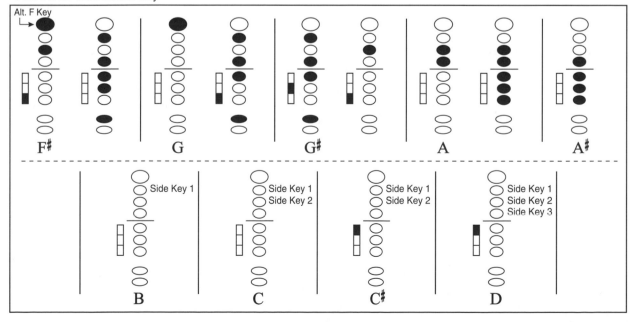

59 HIGH-NOTE EXERCISE

Now that you're comfortable playing high notes with the proper fingerings, let's try an exercise. This high-note exercise requires you to play notes in octaves to the altissimo fingering and back to the regular note. Practice this slowly and with a tuner, making sure to play the altissimo note in tune. Adjust your embouchure to fix the pitch.

TRACK 20

60 THE COLLECTOR'S PIECE!

The Selmer Mark VI was *the* classic horn made between 1956 and 1973. Its metal, craftsmanship, mechanics, and "heart" have all contributed to its reputation as a great horn. These horns play wonderfully and just seem to have the "sound," and that "sound" has never been duplicated; they truly are magical horns!

Like any musical instrument, the Selmer Mark VI has certain serial numbers that are famous for their extra value. Collectors and established players often search out these "vintage" horns, making these sought-after jewels quite valuable. But it's important to remember that not all Mark VI horns are great. Some have intonation problems; some are too dark or too bright (depending on the sound you want). Still others are the victims of bad lacquer jobs, and some just lack that certain sound. Most, however, are great horns.

If you're thinking about picking up one of these classics, here are a few things to keep in mind. First, remember that Mark VI horns are considered professional horns, and they require the utmost love and care. Second, stay away from re-lacquered Mark VI horns. They usually don't have the brightness that they originally had, and they don't have the same metal when new lacquer is applied. This, of course, decreases the value of the horn. So, the uglier, older, beat-up, and crusty-looking the horn, the better! Try out as many as you can to see which one feels and sounds the best to you, and finally, be prepared to shell out between $3000–$7000!

61 ALWAYS USE A METRONOME

If you don't own a metronome, go buy one—now! Solid time is the most important element in playing music (along with playing in tune). You *must* play with good time, and the best way to help your sense of time is to use a metronome. Use it all the time, whether you're practicing scales, patterns, hard passages, or etudes: use it on everything.

There are two types of metronomes: electronic and manual. Electric metronomes are battery-operated and far more inexpensive (as little as $20). Manual metronomes require you to "wind them up," and then a pendulum clicks back and forth. These are generally nicer in appearance and thus more expensive.

The bottom line is that any metronome is good if it helps you develop a good sense of time!

62 CHOOSE THE RIGHT MOUTHPIECE

Choosing the right mouthpiece is the biggest decision you can make for your saxophone playing. It's the mouthpiece that contributes the most to your sound. Here are some things to look for in a mouthpiece:

- Use either a hard rubber or metal mouthpiece. Stay away from plastic or other synthetic materials.

- Make sure it produces a quality tone throughout all registers of the horn.

- Make sure it plays in tune.

- Choose a reputable brand name.

- Make sure to find the right reed brand and strength for the mouthpiece. Certain mouthpieces require certain reeds.

- Ask other players for input on what the mouthpiece sounds like when you play it.

- Don't pay too much money. No mouthpiece is the one you will use forever!

- If you choose a jazz mouthpiece, make sure it's not too edgy or too bright. You want some room for your tone and your sound to grow and improve.

63 MOUTHPIECE ANATOMY

Knowing the inside of the mouthpiece is very important. It will help you understand how they work and sound, which in turn will help you know what to look for in a mouthpiece. This knowledge can also help you decide what alterations the inside of the mouthpiece may need to produce a certain type of sound. Here is a mouthpiece diagram:

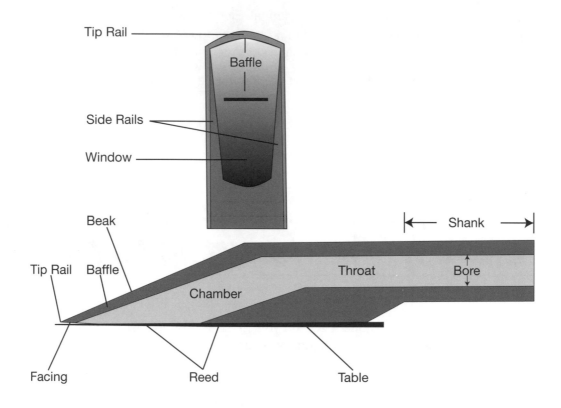

64 DON'T BE A COPYCAT

In other words, don't use a certain type of reed or mouthpiece just because your favorite artist uses it. You will never sound like him or her anyway—no matter how much you try. Everyone's mouth, throat cavity, and lung power is different and unique, just like everyone's speaking voice. You should try to find your own voice and your own sound! It's good to go through periods where you absorb a famous saxophonist's playing and get his or her sound and vocabulary down. But buying a mouthpiece, reed, or even a horn similar to that player just to sound like him or her is simply a waste of money. Instead, spend your time and money finding reeds and mouthpieces that work best for *you*!

65 TRAIN YOUR EARS

Ear training is one of the most valuable things any musician can do to grow and advance. You should train your ears for tuning, note recognition, chord recognition, and to quickly find notes on your saxophone.

If you have bad ears, don't fret. You can train them to listen and hear better. A simple practice method is to play a note on a piano, and try to play it quickly on your instrument. Be sure to vary the range of notes; otherwise you're not truly training your ear. Another great way to train your ears is to get together with another musician and play notes for each other. Try to repeat the note that he or she plays, and vice versa.

Track 21 gives an example of this exercise.

TRACK 21

66 PRACTICE HARD SCALES FIRST

When learning and practicing scales, players tend to always start with the easy ones. Instead, start with the hard scales. For instance, work on C♯ major instead of C major. By practicing scales you already know rather than those you're not comfortable with, you're wasting valuable practice time. And remember, there are no hard scales, just scales you don't know!

67 HOW TO PRACTICE TUNES

A good way to practice tunes is to first play the melody over and over until you have it memorized. Next, learn the changes by outlining the chords on your instrument (playing arpeggios, including any extensions) until you can fully hear the chord quality. Next, go back to playing the melody and try to "hear" the chord changes go by as you play. Try and hear the first note of every chord, in your you head. This will replicate what the bass part usually is. Do this over and over until you have the tune and changes memorized. It's also helpful to find a recording of the song and sing along with the melody and changes.

68 PRACTICE CHANGES WITH A PIANO

A good way to practice chord changes is with a piano. Play a chord with the sustain pedal down, and just practice playing over the chord. Don't worry about your piano playing skills or any specific voicings. Just play the standard block chord voicing (1–3–5–7) and practice the changes. You can hear an example of this in Track 22.

TRACK 22

69 THE MOUTHPIECE CAP

Always leave the mouthpiece cap on the mouthpiece when you're not playing. This keeps your reed from drying out, prevents accidental chips on the reed, as well as protects the mouthpiece rails and tip from being dented or chipped. Even if you drop the mouthpiece, the cap might save it!

If you have a mouthpiece cap that has an open hole on the end, cover it up with some tape. This adds extra covering to help keep the reeds from drying out.

70 THE SCOOP

Note scoops are a way of bending the pitch of a note upward or downward. To bend the pitch down, drop your jaw down. To bend the pitch up, pinch your jaw upward on the reed. Strive to create an even scoop of the pitch. These may feel strange in the beginning, but with practice, scoops become easier to play and control.

Below is a sample melody you can use to practice scoops. Listen to Track 23 to hear how scoops can be practiced on a scale, and then on the melody line shown below.

TRACK 23

71 BUY MUSIC PLAY-ALONGS

Play-alongs are a great way to learn songs, practice your soloing, and help your reading. There are many songbooks containing movie songs, jazz standards, and classics, that come with CDs with which you can jam along. Think of some songs that you like, find a play-along book that has those songs, and play them.

Play-alongs are also great for teaching! They keep the students interested in music by allowing them to play songs that they like along with a band or orchestra.

72 DUCK CALLS?

Practicing with the mouthpiece only is a great way to develop your throat, mouth, and embouchure muscles, as well as your pitch. You may sound a bit like a duck quacking, but this exercise forces you to feel and experiment with different mouth changes—ones that you'll need later for high notes or other tonal variations. Try playing some scales and melodies with the mouthpiece alone, and you'll feel the changes and movements you have to make with your mouth cavity and embouchure.

Practicing with the mouthpiece alone is also a good way to test the flexibility of your mouthpiece.

To hear how practicing with the mouthpiece alone sounds, check out Track 24.

TRACK 24

73   GET SOME EARPLUGS

They're cheap, easy to transport, and absolutely priceless, so why not carry earplugs with you to every gig? You never know when you might need them! You can get a cheap pair of earplugs at any music store. A good and inexpensive type to use are the kind that are pinched and expand when placed in the ear. If you really want to make an investment, you can also buy specially made earplugs that are molded to the shape of your ear canal for a perfect fit. And with these, you can even have certain frequencies raised, lowered, or altered.

Meanwhile, if you don't have earplugs handy and need something in a pinch, get some soft tissue or paper toweling, rip off a small piece, roll it up into a ball, and carefully stick it in your ear. Make sure it's not small enough to get stuck in your ear or hard enough to cut up your inner ear. Remember that you only get one chance to keep your hearing. Once you lose it, you can never gain it back!

74   KEEP A PENCIL IN YOUR CASE

Seems simple, but do you have one in there right now? You should keep a pencil in your case at all times for writing changes in the music, filling out performance or union forms (actually, carry a pen for those), or giving someone your phone number for a future gig. I've been in several situations where the leader makes sudden music changes and expects you to write in those changes. And they certainly don't want to wait around for you find a writing utensil. After all, time is money! So always have a pencil in your case, and keep it nearby.

75   SHED THE SWEET TOOTH

Avoid candy, sodas, beer, and even coffee before playing. These can dirty up your horn and the inside of the mouthpiece, do damage to the pads, and make your reeds look and smell dirty. If you need something, water is always safe. And don't forget to clean your instrument when you're finished playing.

76 "THE ETERNAL TRIANGLE"

If you are comfortable playing "rhythm" changes, which are the changes to the popular standard "I Got Rhythm," try playing Sonny Stitt's "The Eternal Triangle," which has unique changes over the same bridge. First, listen to Track 25 to hear standard "rhythm" changes. Note that these changes are in the key of B♭. You must transpose them for your own instrument.

TRACK 25

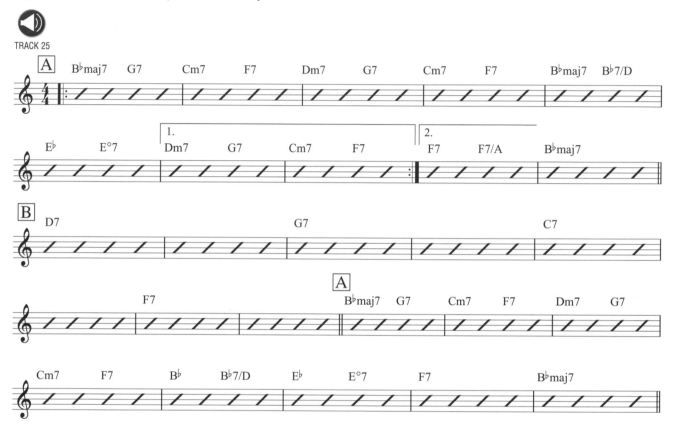

Now, check out Track 26 to hear the changes and altered bridge (a series of ii–Vs descending in half steps) in "The Eternal Triangle."

TRACK 26

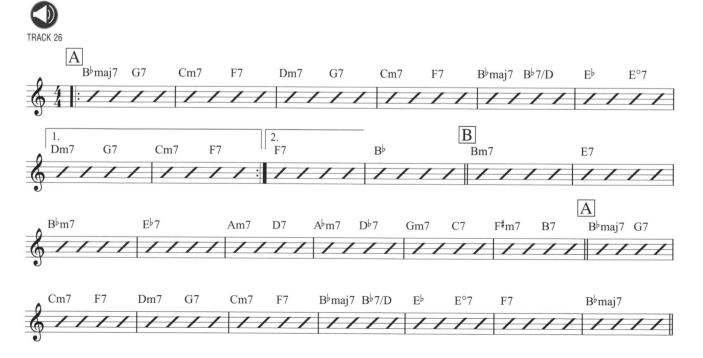

77 TONGUING IT ALL

Saxophone great Dexter Gordon had a jazz articulation technique where he tongued most of his eighth notes during his solos. Check out his recordings to fully understand his melodic style and technical mastery, and try to incorporate his tongue articulation style into your own playing. Track 27 demonstrates this technique using a brief solo over a ii–V–I pattern.

TRACK 27

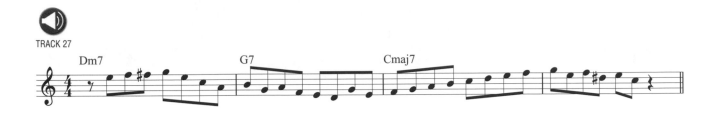

78 HELLO, MY NAME IS ...

In the music business, it's all about whom you know, your attitude, getting your name out there, and being at the right place at the right time—in other words, networking. If you're the shy, quiet type, it's time to overcome it. Whenever you play a gig—particularly when you play well—be sure to mingle and chat with the other players in the band or orchestra as well as those in attendance. Remember, you're selling a product—*you!* And don't forget to hand out your business cards to the right people. Trust me, if you played well and carry a professional and friendly attitude, they'll call.

79 REED ADJUSTMENT

Has there ever been a time when your reed was too soft or too hard to play? Here's a quick way to make a soft, broken-in reed feel stronger or a hard reed feel softer. Simply raise or lower the reed on the mouthpiece, over or under the mouthpiece tip rail. Raising it will strengthen the feel of the reed (as the reed will thicken), and lowering it will weaken its feel (by playing on the thinner part). This is a great shortcut instead of replacing the reed.

Reed higher than
mouthpiece tip rail

Reed lower than
mouthpiece tip rail

80 BREATHE CORRECTLY

Most of the time, when saxophonists take a breath to play, they just fill up their mouths with air. The correct way to breathe is to inhale air all the way down from your diaphragm. Once you start to breathe correctly, your sound will become fuller and bigger, and you'll be able to play longer notes. Are you taking in a little air, or are you really filling up from the bottom of your belly? Chances are, you're not breathing correctly. Practice doing it the correct way, and hear your playing improve!

81 TAKE "GIANT STEPS"

Hopefully you've heard of John Coltrane and his landmark album, *Giant Steps.* If not, do yourself a favor and check out this masterpiece. Coltrane revolutionized jazz and its harmony by introducing a set of chord changes that move in descending major 3rds. He used this amazing concept in his famous tune "Giant Steps," and he used variations of this sequence in many of his other original compositions. There are only four possible ways to play this cycle of key centers that descend by major thirds:

1. Cmaj7–E♭7–A♭maj7–B7–Emaj7–G7–Cmaj7

2. D♭maj7–E7–Amaj7–C7–Fmaj7–A♭7–D♭maj7

3. Dmaj7–F7–B♭maj7–D♭7–G♭maj7–A7–Dmaj7

4. E♭maj7–G♭7–Bmaj7–D7–Gmaj7–B♭7–E♭maj7

The song "Giant Steps" is basically a series of ii–V–I progressions (see Tip 39). The tempo is usually very fast, which makes the song pretty challenging. But it's a very important song to be able to solo on, so practice the changes below slowly with Track 28.

TRACK 28

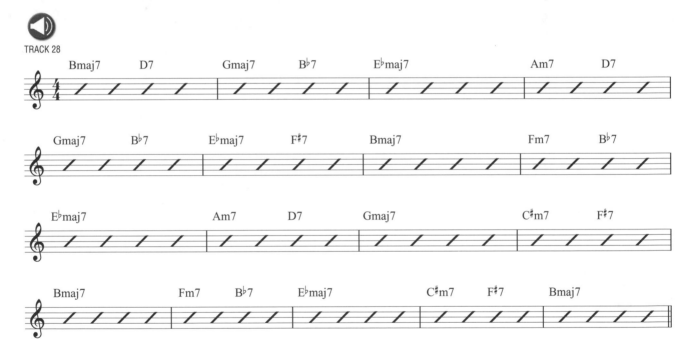

When you feel comfortable with these changes, learn how and where to apply these chord changes to other tunes!

82 CHOOSE THE RIGHT CASE

The right case is an extremely important factor in keeping your "baby" in good shape. That's why it's always worth it to invest in a good case. Here are some things you should consider when looking for a new case or assessing your own current case:

- Make sure your horn fits tightly in the case. To test this, put your horn in the case, close it, and then pick it up and carefully shake it around. The horn shouldn't move. If it does, fill any spaces with bubble wrap or soft foam. Any movement of the instrument can ultimately lead to adjustment issues or worse.

- Apply pressure to the top of the case from every direction and see if it moves. If it does, you're asking for trouble. The case should remain perfectly rigid at all times if you want your instrument to be fully protected.

- Make sure the latches lock securely. If not, a luggage shop can make necessary repairs for you or replace the latches.

- Avoid plastic cases! They're not sturdy; they flex and dent easily, and can warp from heat. Fiberglass cases, although more expensive, are much better.

- Watch out for cases that use ordinary Styrofoam as padding.

- Try to stay away from gig bags! They look nice and are easy to carry around, but they won't protect your horn very well if dropped. If you do decide to use a gig bag, put some extra cloth or padding inside for added protection.

- Ask other saxophonists which cases they use and whether or not they are satisfied with them.

83 PALM KEYS

Sure, you use the palm keys for the high notes, but what about using them for other notes? The palm keys can make certain notes sound more open, less stuffy, and can present an easier alternative for certain fingerings. Here are some other ways you can use the palm keys other than for their normal use:

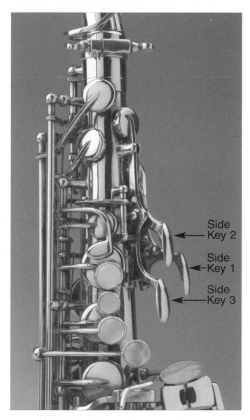

ALTO

Side key 1 or side key 2: Use this side key for the fourth-line D. You will get a cleaner and more open-sounding note.

Side keys 2 and 3: Use these for E♭

Side keys 2, 3, and 4 (which is your right hand E key): Use these for E

TENOR

Side key 1: Use for fourth line D

Side key 1 and side key 2: Use for E♭.

Side keys 1, 2, 3, and 4: Use for E

Experiment with these fingerings, as certain ones will work better on each horn.

84 TRY STRONGER REEDS

Playing with a stronger reed than usual is a good way to strengthen your sound and embouchure muscles, as well as to improve your intonation. Start by moving up one level of reed strength. Your sound will probably become more airy, and you may be forced to play with more air. You'll notice that your chin muscles may also start to get tired. But keep playing, as you're just strengthening the muscles. After a while, you should notice that the hard reeds aren't so hard anymore, and that your sound has become stronger—along with your lungs. So try a harder reed for its benefits, but remember that some mouthpieces require a softer reed.

85 PLAYING FAST

The secret to playing a melody line or soloing fast is to first play something slowly with a metronome, striving to keep good time. Then, when you can play the selected piece or solo in time and cleanly, slowly increase your speed until you reach the desired tempo. For example, take a pattern, melody, or solo that you want to play fast, and first play it at a ballad tempo, say, 60 bpm. Once you can play it perfectly in time, keep the tempo at 60 bpm but play the music in double time, still striving to keep good time. You're now playing the pattern at quarter note = 120! Now turn the metronome up to 120 and play the pattern. If you're really comfortable at that pace, try to play in double time again. If you can do it, you're playing at a Coltranesque 240 bpm! If that's too fast, crank the metronome down to 90 bpm and try double time at that tempo, which is still a whopping 180.

Listen to Track 29 to hear this practice method in action.

TRACK 29

After playing patterns like this, try playing melodies like Charlie Parker's "Confirmation" or "Donna Lee" starting at a slow tempo, and then gradually increasing it. You'll get faster much more quickly and be able to play cleaner using this method rather than jumping right in and trying to play fast right away!

86 PLAY WHAT YOU HEAR

The ultimate goal while soloing in jazz should be to sing or hear what's in your head, and then play it on your horn in that same instant. Or as they say, "singing into your horn."

Getting to this level requires good ear training (Tip 65), knowing what a specific note sounds like and where it is on the horn, and having good control over your horn.

To practice this skill, sing a note out loud, and then immediately try to find it on your instrument. Next, try to sing a melody and play it. You don't need to have a great singing voice; just sing the notes you hear in your head, and then replicate them on your horn.

Remember: Your goal should be to sing what's in your head, and then instantly sing through your instrument. Track 30 is a demonstration of this technique. There is no accompanying notation, as you should use this track as an ear training exercise!

TRACK 30

87 PROTECT THE NECK

Your saxophone neck is very important to the tone and intonation of your saxophone (see Tip 88). Be sure to properly protect the neck while your horn is in its case. You can make sure it doesn't rattle around by securing the neck with bubble wrap or foam in the case or accessory box. If you store the neck in the accessory box, make sure other accessories inside your case don't bang into it.

If you have a gig bag or a flight case, use a padded neck bag or wrap an old sock around the neck, and then place it into the bell of the saxophone.

88 TRY A NEW NECK

You may be surprised to learn that the saxophone's neck makes a huge difference in your sound and intonation. Changing the neck can make your tone mellower, brighter, or darker. It can even help your intonation. Experiment with different brands and sizes of necks to find one that not only fits your horn, but also produces the sound you want.

89 TRANSCRIBE SOLOS

Transcribing solos is a great way to develop your ear training, music reading, rhythm skills, jazz articulation, style characteristics, and the songs themselves. Here are some tips on how to transcribe:

- Pick a song or solo that you really enjoy and would like to learn.
- Start with solos that have easy rhythms and fewer notes, like slow blues tunes.
- Listen to the recording over and over again until you have it memorized and can hear or sing the notes.
- Get some manuscript paper and write out bar lines for the first 8, 12 or 32 bars of the solo.
- Write down the notes you hear, verifying with your horn what they are. Be sure to write them out with the correct rhythms.
- Double-check the notes and rhythms by playing along with the solo.
- Save the solo so you have a record of it to go back to and study in the future.

90 QUIT YOUR JAWING

When playing octaves or making big interval jumps between notes, make sure to keep your jaw still—don't raise or lower it! Moving your jaw not only can alter the pitch of the notes, but also can provide a greater chance for the lower note to crack. If you currently move your jaw or embouchure when playing octaves or wide-interval jumps, spend some time practicing in front of a mirror—it will help.

I guarantee with practice, your low notes will pop out too!

91 STUDIO SESSIONS

Here are some important tips to remember if your goal is to become a successful studio musician:

- Be sure you always play in tune.
- Show up on time or even early.
- Have all the required horns with you and make sure they are in working order.
- Be able to adjust your tone or style to what the leader or producer wants from you (and keep a pencil handy for taking those directions down).
- Keep your sightreading chops up.
- Maintain a positive attitude and always be courteous to the leader and other musicians.
- Always listen to what the other musicians are playing.
- Keep quiet, and only make comments when you are asked.

Finally, be prepared for any situation. And remember, it doesn't hurt to smile. There are studio scenes in every major city. Use these tips, and you'll be a big success!

92 MIND YOUR MINORS

There are three types of minor scales in classical music: natural minor, harmonic minor (see Tip 14), and melodic minor. Let's examine them.

The *natural* minor scale is simply the major scale but with flatted 3rd, 6th, and 7th degrees. For example, to produce an A minor scale, start with A major (A–B–C#–D–E–F#–G#), and then flat the 3rd (C# becomes C), 6th (F# becomes F), and 7th (G# becomes G) notes, resulting in this spelling: A–B–C–D–E–F–G.

TRACK 31

A minor (Natural)

The natural minor is also just the 6th mode of a major scale. In this case, A natural minor has the same notes as C major.

The *harmonic* minor scale is the same as the natural minor scale, except that you do not flat the 7th degree: A–B–C–D–E–F–G#.

TRACK 32

A minor (Harmonic)

The harmonic is also just a natural minor scale, with a raised 7th note!

The *melodic* minor scale is the quirky one of the bunch. The easiest way to remember how to play a melodic minor scale is to play a major scale, only with a flatted 3rd degree: A–B–C–D–E–F#–G#. A melodic minor scale is also just a harmonic minor with a raised 6th and 7th note upwards, lowered back when going down. In classical music, melodic minor has only a flatted 3rd whenever you *ascend* the scale. But when you *descend*, you flat the 3rd, 6th, and 7th; in other words, you play melodic minor on the way up and natural minor on the way down.

TRACK 33

A minor (Melodic)

Learning these scales with their alterations may seem confusing. But with practice and study, they will make important sense.

Another thing to remember about melodic minors: in jazz, the alterations ascending are the same descending. The scale is the same up and down. This is called the jazz melodic minor.

Remember: Practice the three minors in all 12 keys!

93 NECK STRAPS

A good neck strap can save you from future serious neck and back problems—not to mention money on possible instrument repairs! Make sure the neck strap is comfortable, padded, strong, and fits the horn. Also, the strap should have a clip or closed hook on the end. This will keep the neck strap from accidentally unhooking, thus saving the horn from an unexpected fall. Don't be cheap; it's well worth the extra money for a reliable neck strap that will provide you years of comfort and stability in your playing!

94 LEARN HOW TO TRANSPOSE

Learn how to transpose C (piano or guitar) chord changes and melodies to B♭ (tenor or soprano) or E♭ (alto or baritone). As you've already encountered in this book, many times you'll be given parts in C and have to read and transpose those parts on the spot. That's why being able to transpose quickly is a must!

Transposition is something that you can learn easily—with practice. For tenor or soprano sax players, practice reading music up one whole step (read C, play D). For alto or baritone sax, practice reading music down a minor 3rd (read C, play A). It's tough at first, but it will get easier and faster with practice!

95 PRACTICE SOFTLY

The ability to practice softly is quite beneficial when excess volume is an issue. Say, for instance, that you get hired to play a gig with just one day's notice, and you need to practice a few parts the night before. Or how about if you're in a hotel room? You don't want to skip your practice session out of fear of waking the neighbors.

Practicing softly is simple: just play with less air! Obviously, this is not good for working on your tone, but for working on scales or rhythms, it's a valuable skill to have. Listen to Track 34 for a sample of how to practice softly.

TRACK 34

96 PRACTICE LONG TONES

Sure, "long tones" can be long, boring, and may annoy your neighbors, but they are the best exercise for developing your tone and strengthening your embouchure muscles. Practice long tones as a warm-up every time you practice. Start with a low B♭ and play as loud as you can, keeping your embouchure still, and making sure the pitch stays constant—like a straight line. Set your metronome at 60 bpm and move up chromatically, playing two whole notes with only one breath. This not only will help you concentrate on your breathing, but also will increase your lung power. If you notice your embouchure muscles tiring, it means you're doing the exercise correctly. Do it everyday, and your tone will be much bigger and fuller in no time.

TRACK 35

97 BUYING A PROFESSIONAL HORN

Getting to the level where you outgrow or outplay your beginner or intermediate horn means it's time to upgrade to a better horn. Some things to consider when moving to a professional horn include how long you've been playing sax, the sound quality you're getting from your current horn (are you overpowering it?), the physical aspects of a new horn, and finally, the cost of a new instrument.

A professional horn will have better-quality metal, superb craftsmanship, and provide better intonation. Plus, it will just "feel" better, technically. There are many professional horns from which to choose (Selmer, Guardala, Yamaha, and Yanagasawa are a few). Play and experiment with these horns to hear and feel the differences. The costs of these horns also will be a factor, as professional horns are more expensive. In the long run though, a professional horn is a great investment if you plan on playing the instrument for many years!

98 ID, PLEASE

Place labels or ID tags on *everything* (your horn cases, music stands, books, music bags, etc.). You can use mailing labels, but a good, sturdy ID tag is best. It should contain your name, address, and correct phone number, so if any of your gear is ever lost or stolen and then recovered, you can be contacted.

Also, don't forget to keep a log somewhere in your home that contains all of your instruments' serial numbers. If they're ever lost or stolen, you'll have a record!

99 BUILD YOUR REPERTOIRE

Building your repertoire of songs makes you a better musician in the long run. Learning jazz standards, pop songs, classic oldies, waltzes, and rock songs with famous horn lines will help prepare you for almost any gigging or recording situation. And whenever you come across a song on a gig that you didn't know on call, make a note of it and learn it for next time. Chances are there will be a next time! Tip 100 gives you a sample list of songs you should know.

100 DON'T BLOW THESE OFF

Here is a short list of songs you should know:

JAZZ STANDARDS

"Have You Met Miss Jones"
"Satin Doll"
"Don't Get Around Much Anymore"
"Summertime"
"New York, New York"
"Take the A Train"
"My Favorite Things"
"I Got Rhythm"

BALLADS

"At Last"
"My Funny Valentine"
"Misty"

"In a Sentimental Mood"
"Unforgettable"
"When I Fall in Love"
"Autumn in New York"
"My One and Only Love"
"Stardust"

BOSSA NOVA

"Wave"
"The Girl From Ipanema"
"Corvacado"
"Blue Bossa"
"Meditation"

SAFE SAX

Here are some things you should have with you just in case there's ever a horn emergency:

- Black electrical tape: tape up broken keys, or replace missing cork or felts.
- Rubber bands: replace broken springs.
- Small screwdrivers: tighten loose screws or key stoppers.
- Garbage bag ties: fix broken or lost screws for rods.
- Blue poster glue: fix missing corks or felts (with a small piece of paper to avoid sticking).
- Earplugs: for those unexpected gigs where the volume becomes ear-piercing.
- Extra reeds: when the weather or room climates affect the reed adversely.
- Pencil: a must for corrections or changes in the music.
- Yamaha Powder Paper: helps stop sticky pads.
- Key oil: periodically oil up the keys and rods.
- Reed cutter: cut reeds to make them softer.
- Sheet of cork: replace any missing or loose cork.

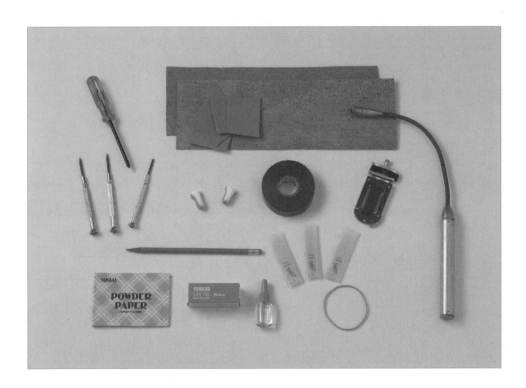

ARTIST TRANSCRIPTIONS®

Artist Transcriptions are authentic, note-for-note transcriptions of the hottest artists in jazz, pop, and rock today. These outstanding, accurate arrangements are in an easy-to-read format which includes all essential lines. Artist Transcriptions can be used to perform, sequence or reference.

GUITAR & BASS

The Guitar Style of George Benson 00660113 .....$14.95	Allan Holdsworth – Reaching for the Uncommon Chord 00604049 .....$14.95
The Guitar Book of Pierre Bensusan 00699072 .....$19.95	Leo Kottke – Eight Songs 00699215 .....$14.95
Ron Carter – Acoustic Bass 00672331 .....$16.95	Wes Montgomery – Guitar Transcriptions 00675536 .....$17.95
Stanley Clarke Collection 00672307 .....$19.95	Joe Pass Collection 00672353 .....$18.95
Al Di Meola – Cielo E Terra 00604041 .....$14.95	John Patitucci 00673216 .....$14.95
Al Di Meola – Friday Night in San Francisco 00660115 .....$14.95	Django Reinhardt Anthology 00027083 .....$14.95
Al Di Meola – Music, Words, Pictures 00604043 .....$14.95	The Genius of Django Reinhardt 00026711 .....$10.95
Kevin Eubanks Guitar Collection 00672319 .....$19.95	Django Reinhardt – A Treasury of Songs 00026715 .....$12.95
The Jazz Style of Tal Farlow 00673245 .....$19.95	Johnny Smith Guitar Solos 00672374 .....$16.95
Bela Fleck and the Flecktones 00672359 Melody/Lyrics/Chords $18.95	Mike Stern Guitar Book 00673224 .....$16.95
David Friesen – Years Through Time 00673253 .....$14.95	Mark Whitfield 00672320 .....$19.95
Best of Frank Gambale 00672336 .....$22.95	Jack Wilkins – Windows 00673249 .....$14.95
Jim Hall – Jazz Guitar Environments 00699389 Book/CD $19.95	Gary Willis Collection 00672337 .....$19.95
Jim Hall – Exploring Jazz Guitar 00699306 .....$17.95	

SAXOPHONE

Julian "Cannonball" Adderly Collection 00673244 .....$19.95	The Coleman Hawkins Collection 00672523 .....$19.95
Michael Brecker 00673237 .....$19.95	Joe Henderson – Selections from "Lush Life" & "So Near So Far" 00673252 .....$19.95
Michael Brecker Collection 00672429 .....$19.95	Best of Joe Henderson 00672330 .....$22.95
The Brecker Brothers... And All Their Jazz 00672351 .....$19.95	Best of Kenny G 00673239 .....$19.95
Best of the Brecker Brothers 00672447 .....$19.95	Kenny G – Breathless 00673229 .....$19.95
Benny Carter Plays Standards 00672315 .....$22.95	Kenny G – Classics in the Key of G 00672462 .....$19.95
Benny Carter Collection 00672314 .....$22.95	Kenny G – Faith: A Holiday Album 00672485 .....$14.95
James Carter Collection 00672394 .....$19.95	Kenny G – The Moment 00672373 .....$19.95
John Coltrane – Giant Steps 00672349 .....$19.95	Kenny G – Paradise 00672516 .....$14.95
John Coltrane – A Love Supreme 00672494 .....$12.95	Joe Lovano Collection 00672326 .....$19.95
John Coltrane Plays "Coltrane Changes" 00672493 .....$19.95	James Moody Collection – Sax and Flute 00672372 .....$19.95
Coltrane Plays Standards 00672453 .....$19.95	The Frank Morgan Collection 00672416 .....$19.95
John Coltrane Solos 00673233 .....$22.95	The Art Pepper Collection 00672301 .....$19.95
Paul Desmond Collection 00672328 .....$19.95	Sonny Rollins Collection 00672444 .....$19.95
Paul Desmond – Standard Time 00672454 .....$19.95	David Sanborn Collection 00675000 .....$16.95
Stan Getz 00699375 .....$18.95	The Lew Tabackin Collection 00672455 .....$19.95
Stan Getz – Bossa Novas 00672377 .....$19.95	Stanley Turrentine Collection 00672334 .....$19.95
Stan Getz – Standards 00672375 .....$17.95	Ernie Watts Saxophone Collection 00673256 .....$18.95

PIANO & KEYBOARD

Monty Alexander Collection 00672338 .....$19.95	Hampton Hawes 00672438 .....$19.95
Monty Alexander Plays Standards 00672487 .....$19.95	Ahmad Jamal Collection 00672322 .....$22.95
Kenny Barron Collection 00672318 .....$22.95	Brad Mehldau Collection 00672476 .....$19.95
The Count Basie Collection 00672520 .....$19.95	Thelonious Monk Plays Jazz Standards – Volume 1 00672390 .....$19.95
Warren Bernhardt Collection 00672364 .....$19.95	Thelonious Monk Plays Jazz Standards – Volume 2 00672391 .....$19.95
Cyrus Chesnut Collection 00672439 .....$19.95	Thelonious Monk – Intermediate Piano Solos 00672392 .....$14.95
Billy Childs Collection 00673242 .....$19.95	Jelly Roll Morton – The Piano Rolls 00672433 .....$12.95
Chick Corea – Elektric Band 00603126 .....$15.95	Michel Petrucciani 00673226 .....$17.95
Chick Corea – Paint the World 00672300 .....$12.95	Bud Powell Classics 00672371 .....$19.95
Bill Evans Collection 00672365 .....$19.95	Bud Powell Collection 00672376 .....$19.95
Bill Evans – Piano Interpretations 00672425 .....$19.95	André Previn Collection 00672437 .....$19.95
The Bill Evans Trio 00672510 Volume 1: 1959-1961 .....$24.95 00672511 Volume 2: 1962-1965 .....$24.95 00672512 Volume 3: 1968-1974 .....$24.95 00672513 Volume 4: 1979-1980 .....$24.95	Gonzalo Rubalcaba Collection 00672507 .....$19.95 Horace Silver Collection 00672303 .....$19.95
The Benny Goodman Collection 00672492 .....$16.95	Art Tatum Collection 00672316 .....$22.95
Benny Green Collection 00672329 .....$19.95	Art Tatum Solo Book 00672355 .....$19.95
Vince Guaraldi Jazz Transcriptions 00672486 .....$19.95	Billy Taylor Collection 00672357 .....$24.95
Herbie Hancock Collection 00672419 .....$19.95	McCoy Tyner 00673215 .....$16.95
Gene Harris Collection 00672446 .....$19.95	Cedar Walton Collection 00672321 .....$19.95
	The Teddy Wilson Collection 00672434 .....$19.95

CLARINET

Buddy De Franco Collection 00672423 .....$19.95

TROMBONE

J.J. Johnson Collection 00672332 .....$19.95

FLUTE

Eric Dolphy Collection 00672379 .....$19.95
James Newton – Improvising Flute 00660108 .....$14.95
The Lew Tabackin Collection 00672455 .....$19.95

TRUMPET

The Chet Baker Collection 00672435 .....$19.95	Miles Davis – Standards Vol. 1 00672450 .....$19.95
Randy Brecker 00673234 .....$17.95	Miles Davis – Standards Vol. 2 00672449 .....$19.95
The Brecker Brothers...And All Their Jazz 00672351 .....$19.95	The Dizzy Gillespie Collection 00672479 .....$19.95
Best of the Brecker Brothers 00672447 .....$19.95	Freddie Hubbard 00673214 .....$14.95
Miles Davis – Originals Volume 1 00672448 .....$19.95	Tom Harrell Jazz Trumpet 00672382 .....$19.95
Miles Davis – Originals Volume 2 00672451 .....$19.95	The Chuck Mangione Collection 00672506 .....$19.95

FOR MORE INFORMATION, SEE YOUR LOCAL MUSIC DEALER, OR WRITE TO:

HAL•LEONARD® CORPORATION
7777 W. BLUEMOUND RD. P.O. BOX 13819 MILWAUKEE, WI 53213

Prices and availability subject to change without notice.
Some products may not be available outside the U.S.A.

Visit our web site for a complete listing of our titles with songlists.
www.halleonard.com

0104